# Zen Munchkins

# Zen Munchkins
## —LITTLE WISDOMS—

compiled by
D.T. Munda

illustrations by J.C. Brown

CHARLES E. TUTTLE COMPANY
Rutland, Vermont & Tokyo, Japan

Published by the Charles E. Tuttle Company, Inc.
of Rutland, Vermont & Tokyo, Japan
with editorial offices at
2-6 Suido 1-chome, Bunkyo-ku, Tokyo 112

© 1991 by Charles E. Tuttle Publishing Co., Inc.

All rights reserved

LCC Card No. 91-65236
ISBN 0-8048-1640-9

First edition, 1991


Printed in Japan

*For*
*Graham*

# Introduction

THE PURPOSE OF THIS BOOK IS TO PRESENT AN overview of wisdom from the past and present that speaks to the spirit of man, both now and as we undergo the great change in consciousness that will accompany our approach to the year 2000.

It has taken me twenty-one years to research this book. In all of my reading, studying, and meditating I have culled from certain books *Wisdom* that seemed to stand up, to jump out at me and to mesh perfectly with other gems I had read at other times. Of course, because: The truth . . . is one. Realizing this, I felt compelled to collect all these "Zen Munchkins," or "little wisdoms," together in one volume. It may be read from beginning to end or opened at random. The result is the same: you will be rewarded with a bit of wisdom that speaks quietly to the inner person—to the soul and spirit.

Enjoy.

—D. T. MUNDA
The Capstone Foundation

THE MAGNETIC INFLUENCE OF THE SUBTLE spheres knows no barriers or frontiers or distance or any other conventional limitation. Whether they desire it or not all persons constantly act and interact upon each other, even when not expressed in word or deed. The world of mental life is as much a unified system as the world of matter.

*

Though he begins by seeking something new
He arrives at the understanding
of
An ancient thing.

\*

Although the clear light of reality shines
Within one's own mind
The multitude look for it elsewhere.

Wondrous is this.

\*

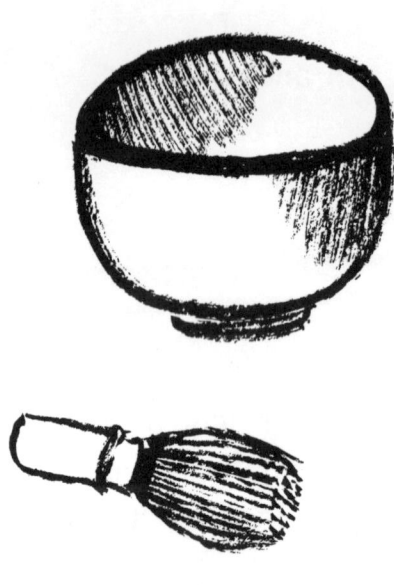

Spiritual ignorance is often so complete that
People do not realize that they are ignorant.

*

In spirituality what matters
Is not theory
But practice.

*

Meditation yields its significance
After the person has experienced it
Not when he tries
To understand it by means of examination.

He should be prepared to encounter
Unexpected states of consciousness
And be willing
To go where he is led
Without expectations.

In spiritual life
Even a sincere mistake
*Taken seriously*
May have more value
Than half-hearted allegiance to theoretical truth.

If the inner life is to be harmonious and enlightened
Divine qualities
Have to be developed and expressed in
Daily life.

\*

To find god

Is to come to one's own self.

\*

The gravitational pull exercised by the heavenly bodies
Upon each other is an expression of love.


Love is the most effective path.


Love and longing for the
Divine object.

There
Are
Those
Who
Believe
Themselves
To
Be
What
They
Are
Not

And
Think
They
Know
When
They
Do
Not.

THE PROCESS OF PERCEPTION OF REALITY RUNS parallel with the process of creation, and the reversing of the process of perception *without* obliterating consciousness amounts to realizing the nothingness of the universe.

*

There is no point in lamenting the world.
There is no point in trying to change the world.
It is incapable of change because
It is merely an effect.

Change your thoughts about the world.
Here you are changing the cause.
The effect will change automatically.

The manifoldness of creation
    And the separateness of individuals

    Exist

Only in imagination.

The spirit and soul are in the mind of the father.
All souls created have a living bond with him.
They are companions in eternity
And were created as such.

I am infinite.

*

The impetus in the absolute
Is to be regarded as a will to be conscious—
An inexplicable
Spontaneous
And sudden impulse.

Attitudes
Are the means
By which
        The creative mind

        Trains the emotions.

\*

Attitudes are consciously chosen.

\*

If you can always forgive one another

You
Can always change.

\*

Selfishness

Inevitably leads to dissatisfaction
And
Disappointment

Because . . .

*Desires are endless.*

\*

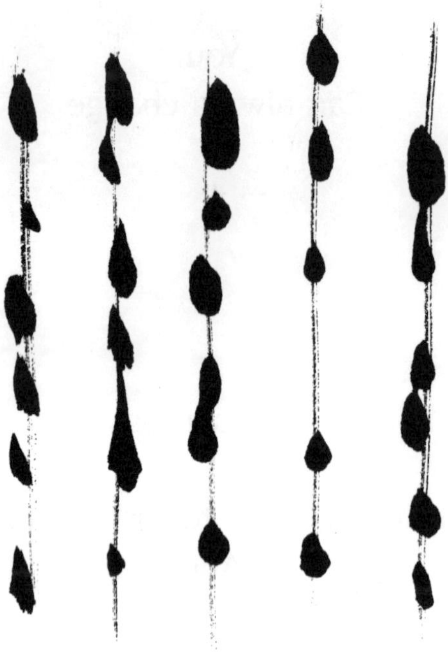

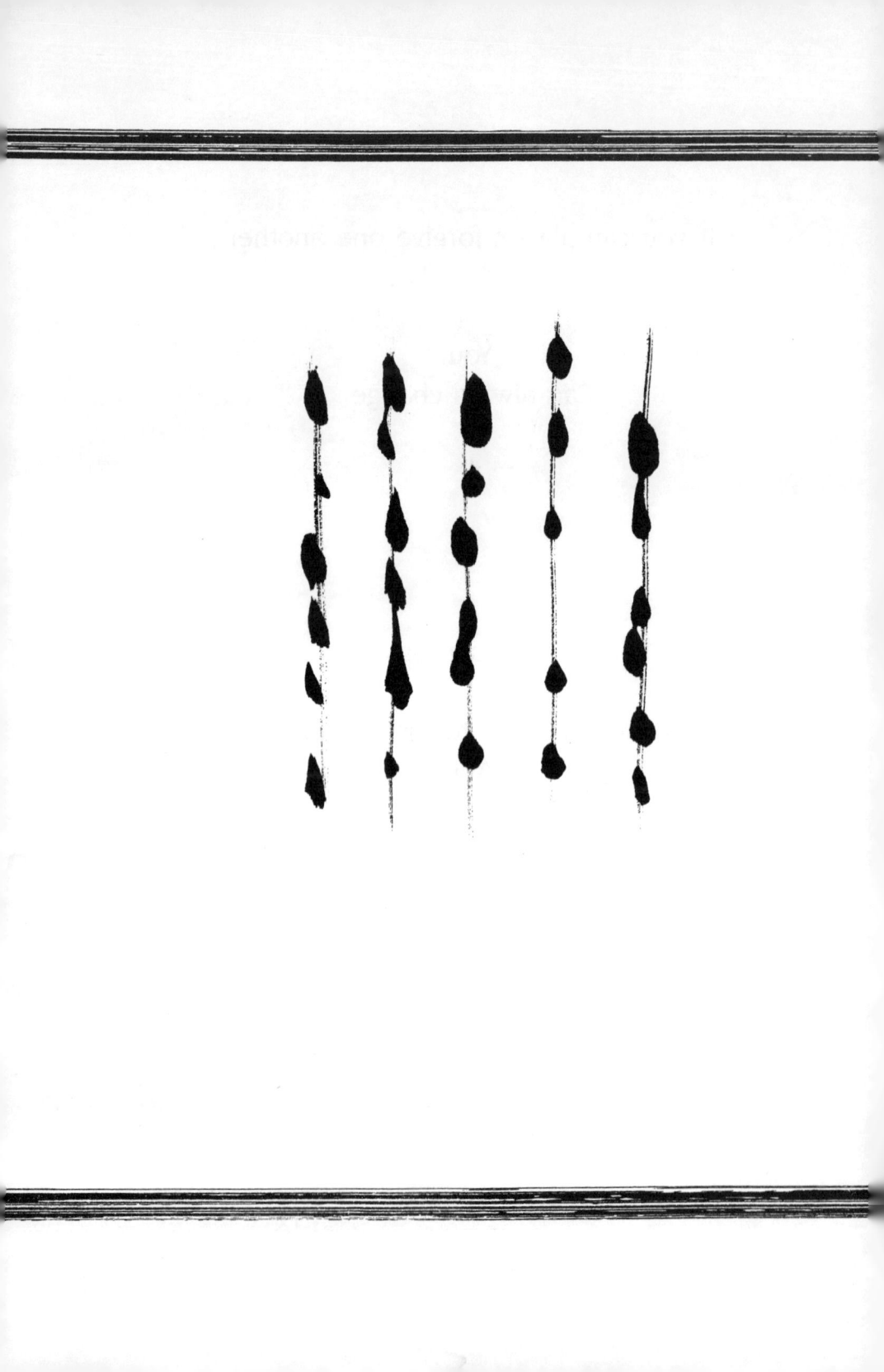

Changes in one's train of thought
    Produce corresponding changes in one's concept
      Of the external world.

*

Various views concerning things
    Are due merely to

        Different

        Mental concepts.

*

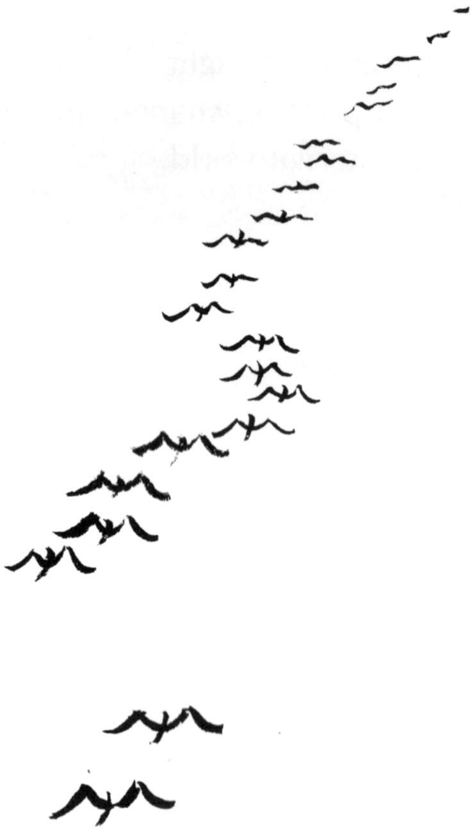

It is better to study god than to be ignorant about him.
It is better to feel for god than to study him.
It is better to experience god than to feel for him.
It is better to become god than to experience him.

*

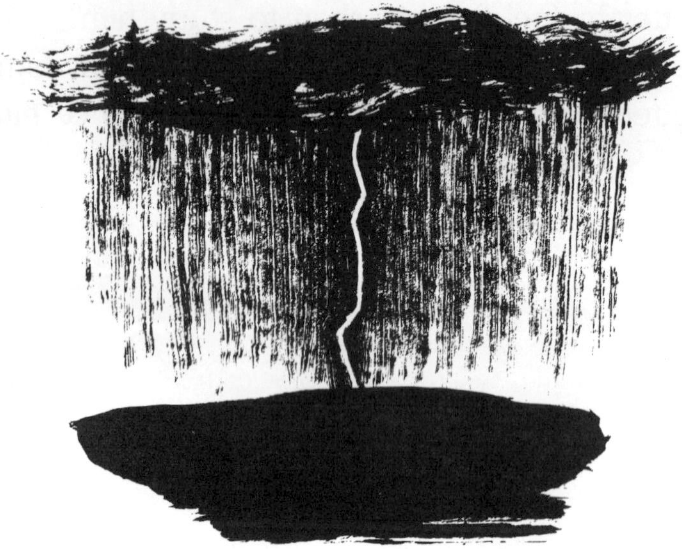

If you are at peace with your fellow man
You are at peace with your god.

\*

Nothing changes that has lasting value.

\*

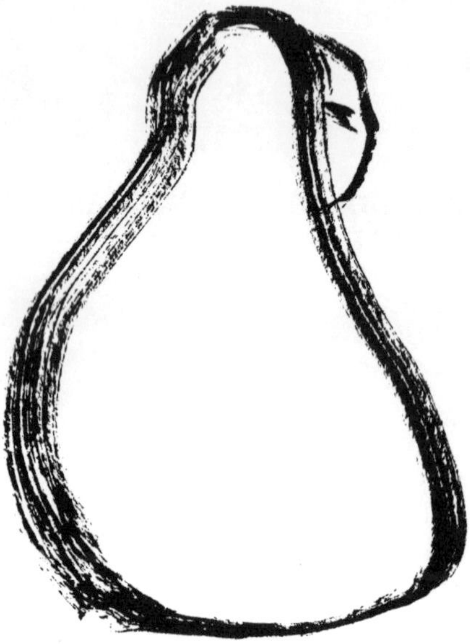

Lust, greed, and anger respectively have
Body, heart, and mind
As their vehicles of expression.
Selfishness seeks fulfillment
Through desires
But succeeds only in increasing
Unsatisfied desires.

*

禅

Can a blind man lead a blind man?
Why do you see the splinter in your brother's eye
And do not see
The beam in your own eye?

*

> Self-knowledge
> Comes to the soul
> By looking
> Within.

*

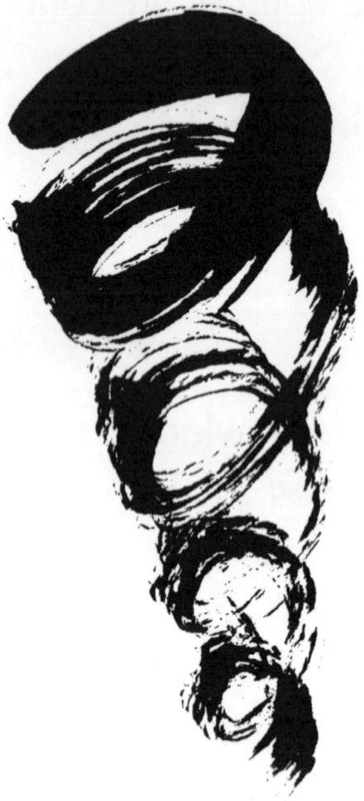

Seek a reality deeper than the changing forms.

*

See yourself in everything, for the universal mind
Includes

All minds.

*

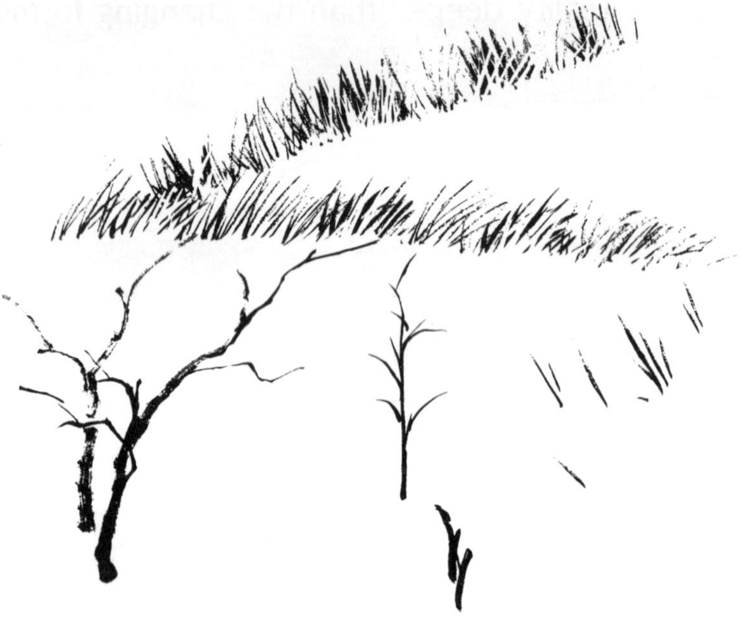

The
Secrets
Of
Spiritual
Life
Are
Opened
To
Those
Who
Venture

        Not
        To
        Those
        Who
        Seek
        Guarantees
        For
        Every
        Step.

          *

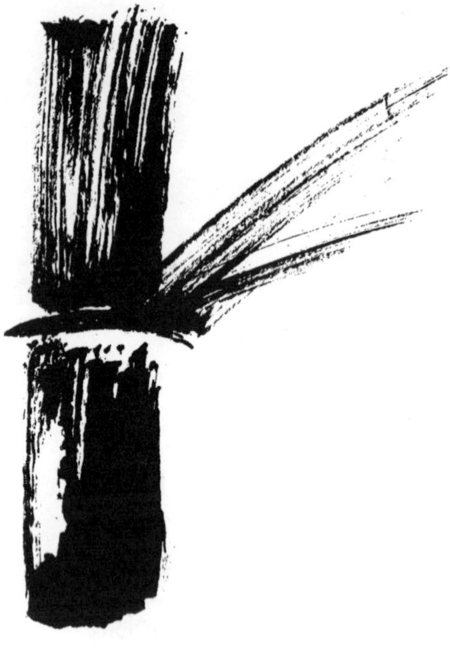

EVERYDAY LIFE HAS TO BE GUIDED BY discrimination and inspired by intuition. The path of action consists in acting upon the intuitions of the heart without hesitation.

\*

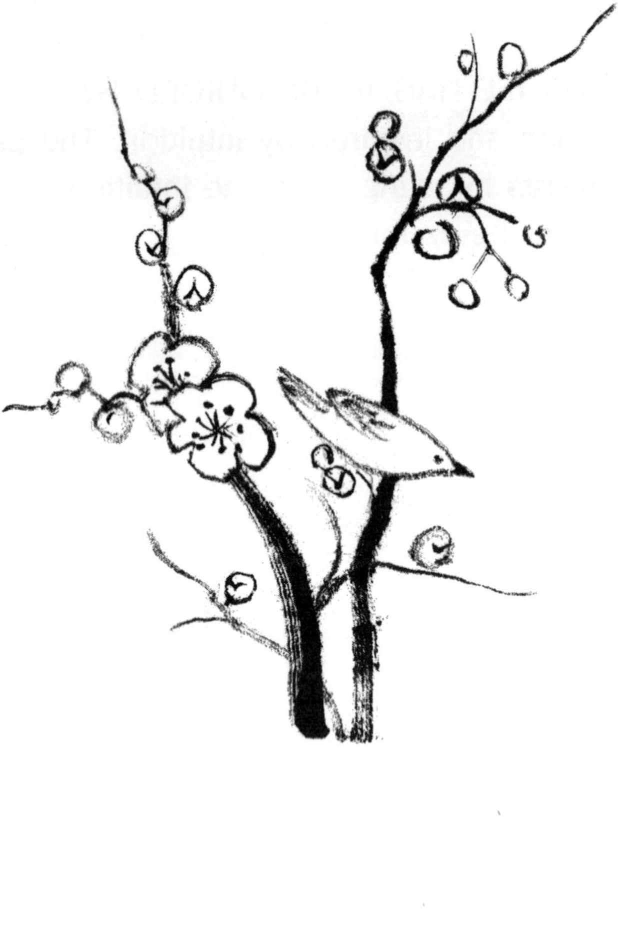

Love is its own reason for being.
It is complete in itself.

When love is present
The path to truth is joyous.

In love, all is spontaneous.
Spontaneity belongs to spirituality.
The state of unlimited spontaneity,
In which there is uninterrupted

Self-knowledge.

*

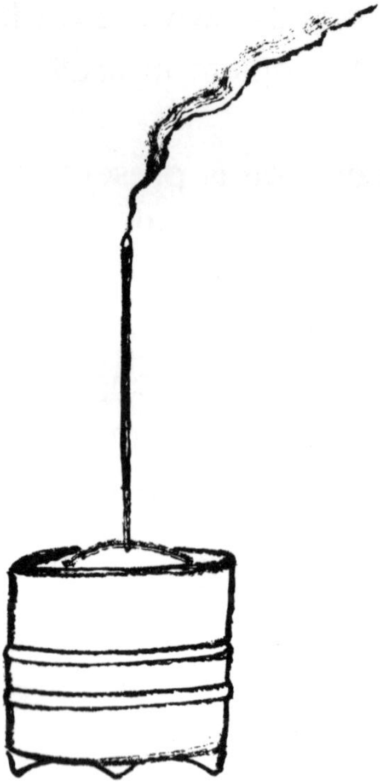

The things of this world are passing
And to cling to them
Is bound to be a source
Of pain.

*

道

True happiness begins
When a man learns the art
Of right adjustment
To other persons

And right adjustment involves

Self-forgetfulness
And
Love.

*

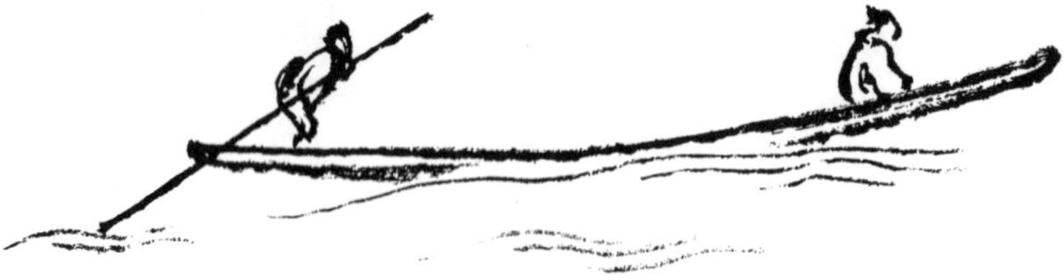

People hold beliefs as they wear
Clothes.

\*

Disappointment
Is an emotional state
Rooted

In self pity.

\*

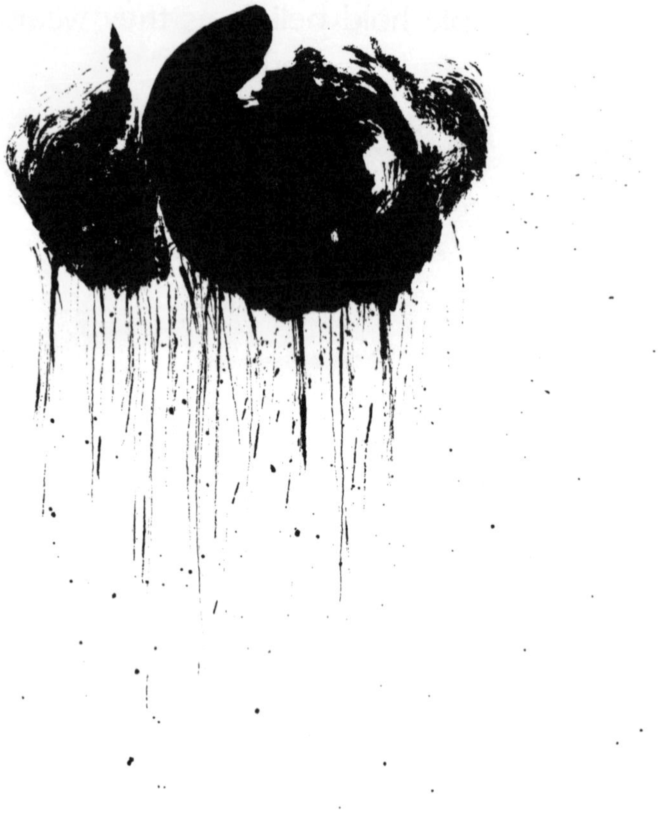

Social problems
Are the effects of men's ideas about
Themselves.

The attitude of men in all these practical
Affairs would be transformed were they
To understand

What was real and what was illusion.

*

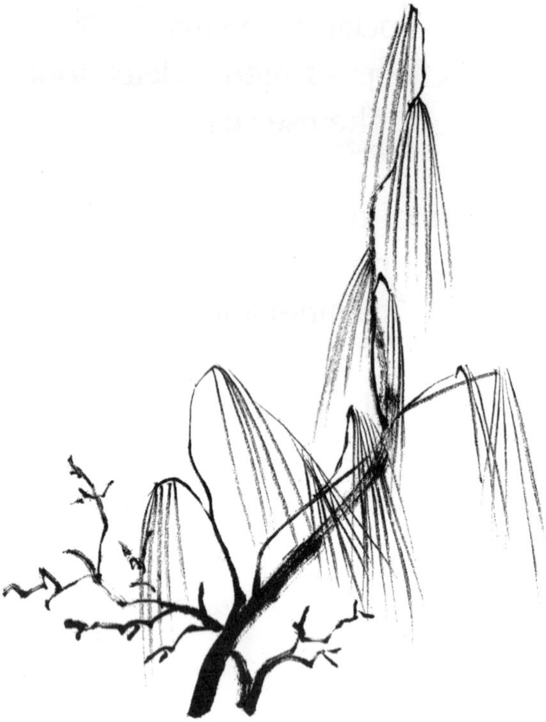

Love the world
As your own self
Then you can truly
Care for all things.

\*

It is more important
To see the simplicity
To realize one's true nature
To cast off selfishness
And temper desire.

\*

Creating yet not possessing
Working yet not taking credit
Work is done then forgotten
Therefore it lasts forever.

\*

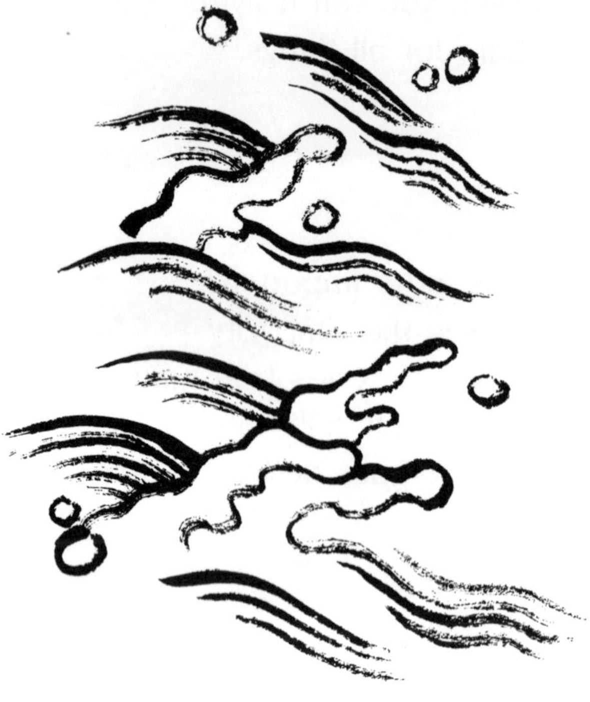

In
The
Universe
Of
Worlds
Earth
Is
As
A
Grain
Of
Sand
On
An
Endless
Eternal
Beach.

*

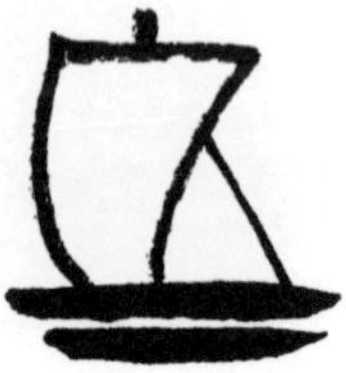

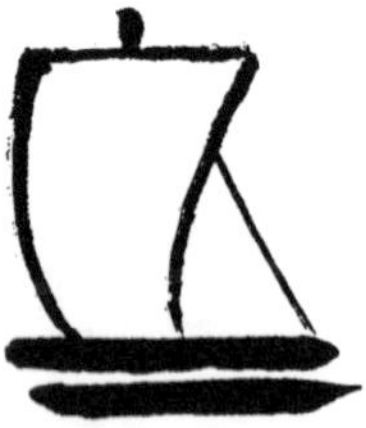

The journey to god
Is merely the reawakening
Of the knowledge of where you are always,
Of what you are forever.

    It is a journey without distance
    To a goal that has never changed.

*

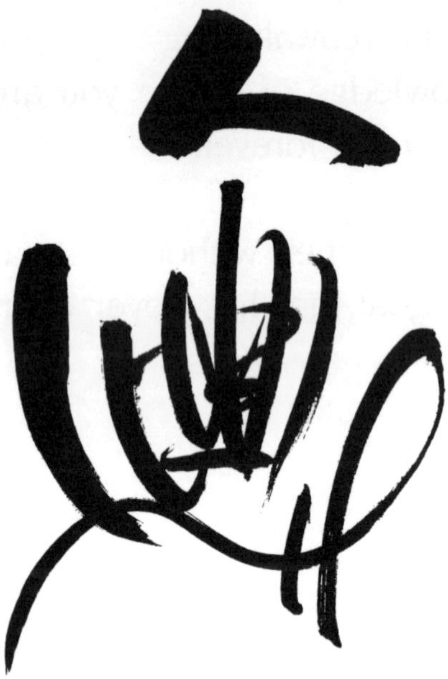

You create reality
Through your feelings
        Thoughts
        And mental actions.

Each mental act
    Is a reality

For which you are responsible.

*

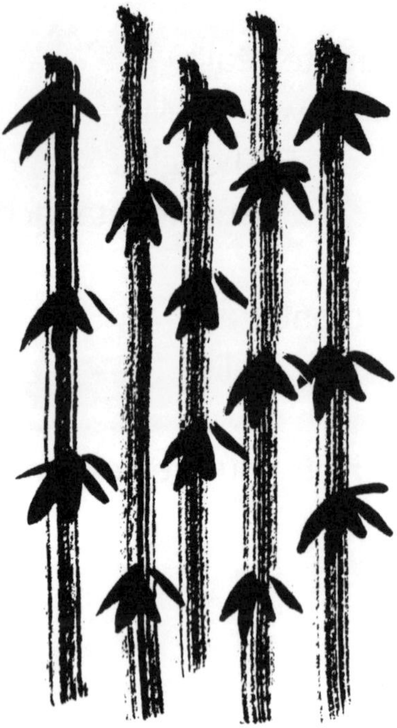

When this mind
Functions in its awesome dignity
Not one deluded thought
May enter
Not one discriminating idea
Can exist.

*

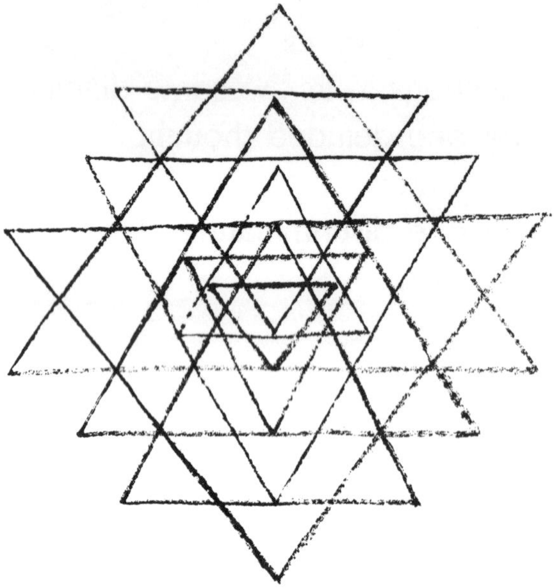

Escaping from the cosmic illusion
And realizing your identity
With the infinite
Is the goal of the long journey.

The path begins
When the soul finds itself
And turns its consciousness toward
The eternal self.

*

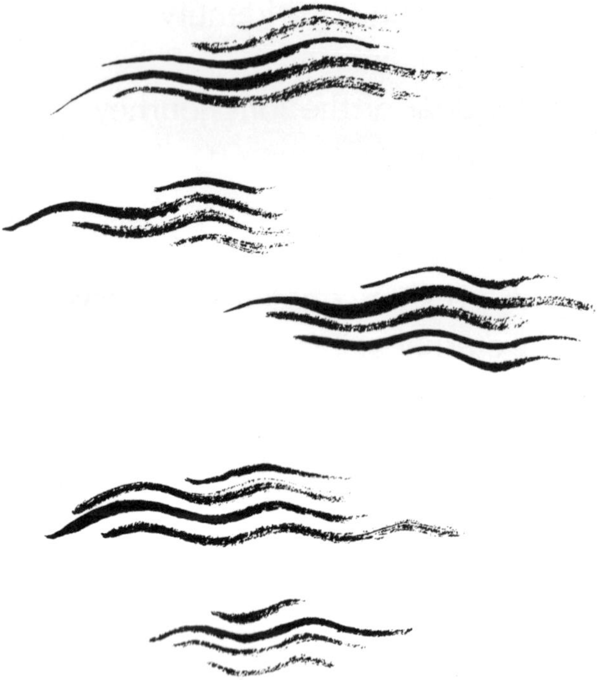

The soul knows itself to be formless
And beyond all the bodies
And worlds
And realizes its unity
With the eternal self.


It
Enjoys
Infinite
Bliss
Peace
Power
And
Knowledge.

\*

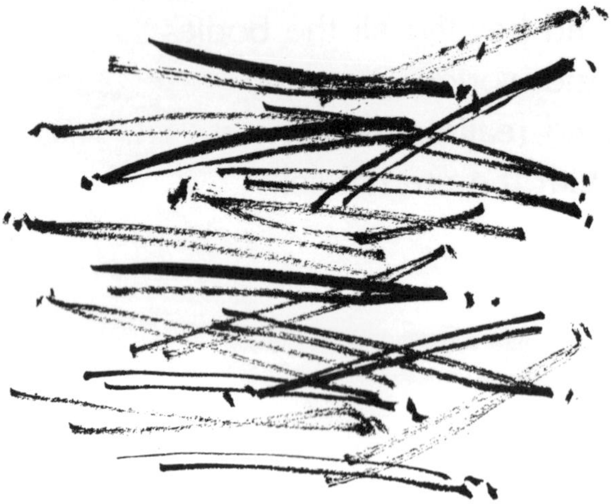

Real knowledge is not found in knowing but in

Being.

*

Attachment to the objects of this world
Is the cause of misery.

*

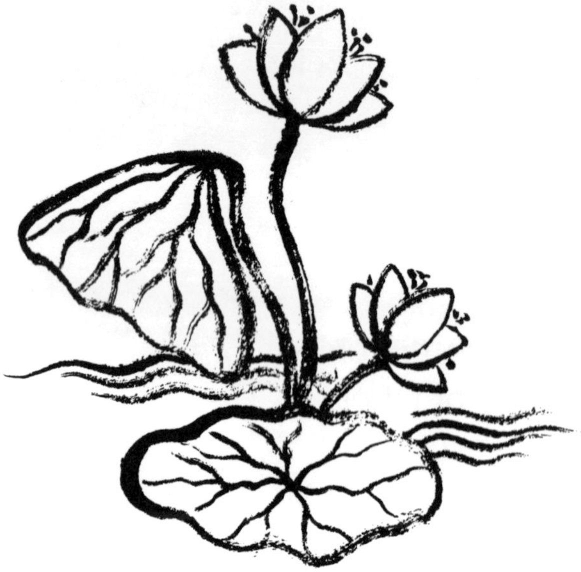

Come, consider the world
A painted chariot for kings
A trap for fools.
But he who sees
Goes free.

*

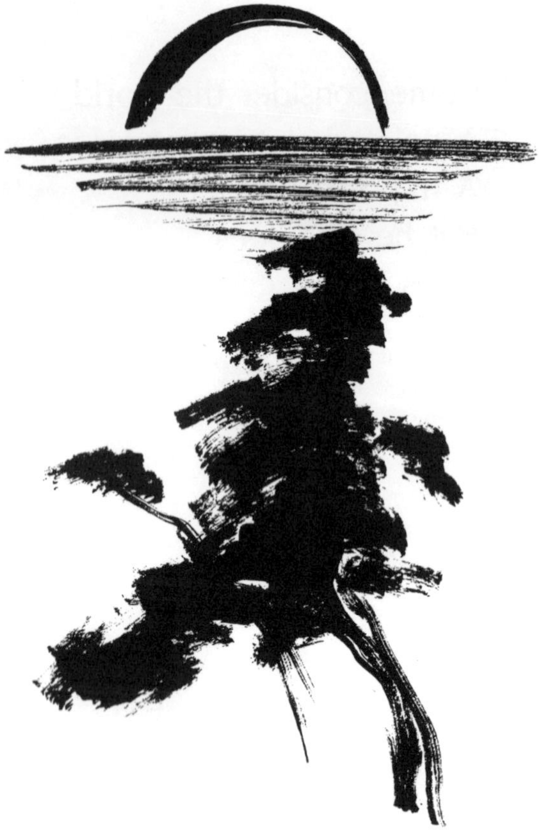

We are what we think.
All that we are
Arises with our thoughts.
With our thoughts
We make the world.

Speak or act with a pure mind
And happiness will follow you
As your shadow
Unshakable.

*

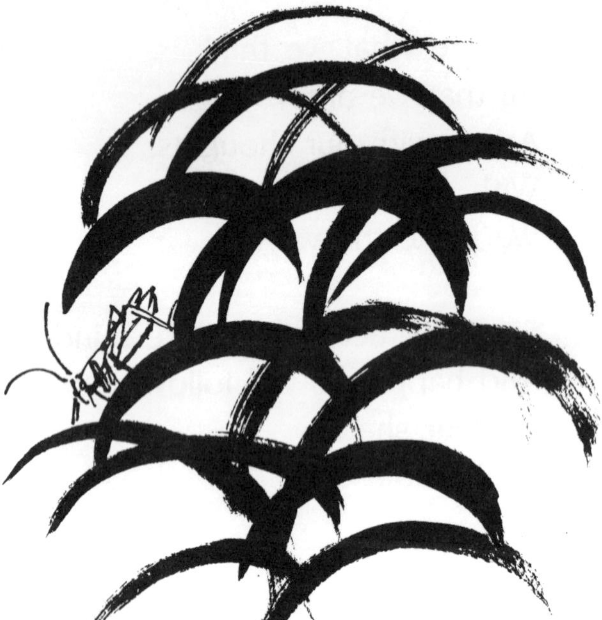

True oneness with god
Is the product
Not of effort on behalf of oneself
Or because of one's own innate goodness

But of love's becoming great enough
To willingly lose itself
On behalf of others.

*

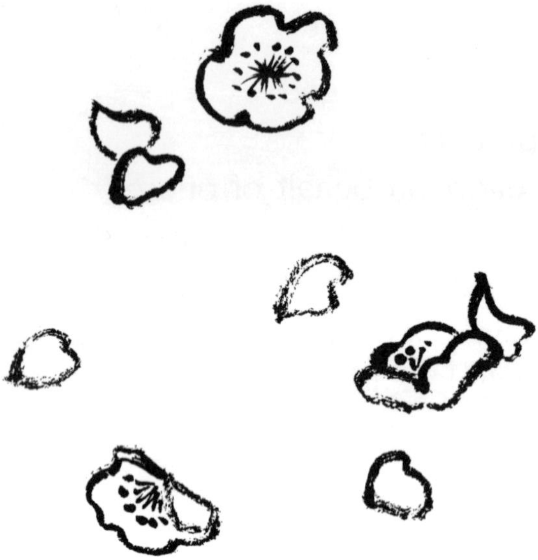

To willingly lose oneself
In love
Is to find oneself
In god.

By its very nature
Such a love uplifts our fellow beings
And creates a greater tendency toward

Peace
And goodwill
Toward all people

\*

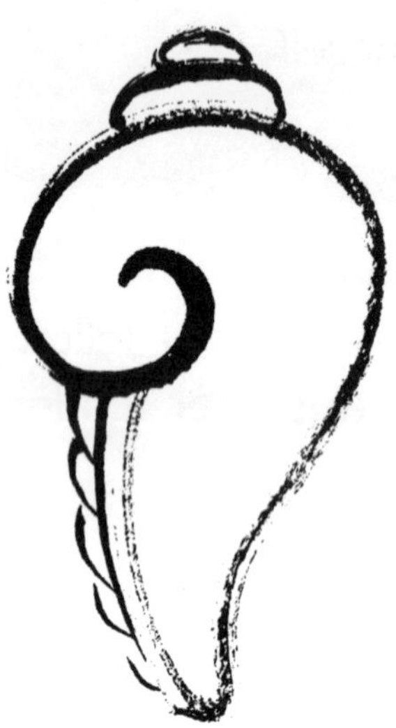

There will be a feeling within you
You will feel a separation
You will know a oneness.

And you will awaken
And you will speak
And your actions will transform the world
And your love
Will reach into the core of all things.

Some will be afraid.
Let them know this great love
Through you

Speak out
Take action
Without
And within.

*

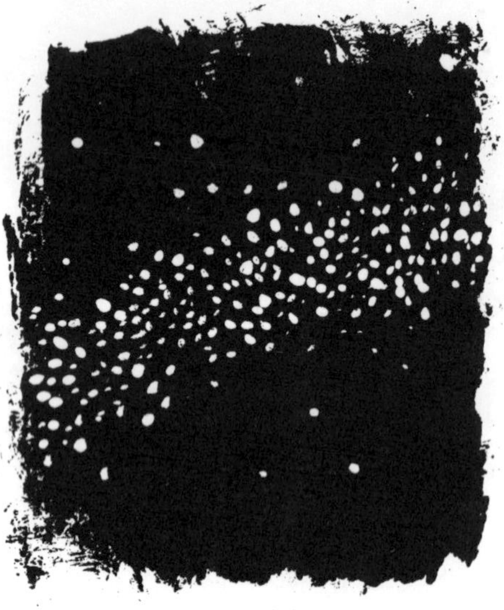

O people of the earth
Men born and made with the elements
But with the spirit of the divine man within you
Rise from your sleep of ignorance!
Realize that your home is not in the earth
But in the light.

*

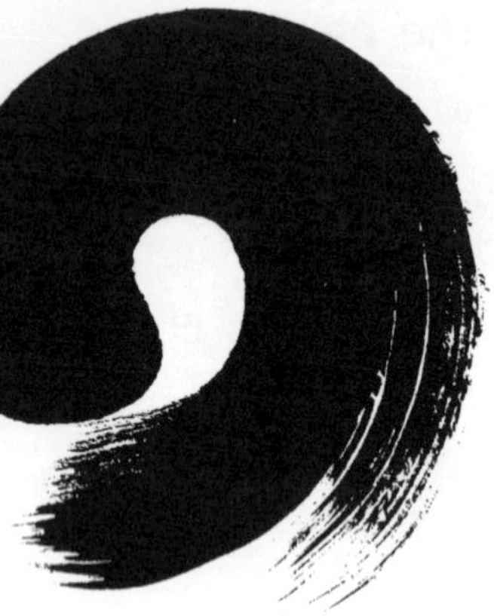

Love
Is not the product
Of any particular religion.
It is the rightful province
Of each and every
Human heart.

*

## Sources

| Page | | Page | |
|---|---|---|---|
| 9 | Meher Baba | 49 | Meher Baba |
| 11 | Meher Baba | 51 | Meher Baba |
| 11 | Padmasambhava | 53 | Meher Baba |
| 13 | Meher Baba | 55 | Meher Baba |
| 15 | Meher Baba | 57 | Meher Baba |
| 17 | Meher Baba | 59 | Meher Baba |
| 19 | Meher Baba | 61 | Meher Baba |
| 21 | Meher Baba | 63 | Lao Tsu |
| 23 | Meher Baba | 65 | Anonymous |
| 25 | A Course in Miracles | 67 | A Course in Miracles |
| 27 | Meher Baba | 69 | Seth |
| 29 | Anonymous | 71 | Hakuin |
| 29 | The Bible | 73 | Meher Baba |
| 31 | Meher Baba | 75 | Meher Baba |
| 33 | Meher Baba | 77 | Swami Rama |
| 35 | Anonymous | 77 | Meher Baba |
| 35 | Meher Baba | 79 | Buddha |
| 37 | Meher Baba | 81 | Buddha |
| 39 | Meher Baba | 83 | Ray Stanford |
| 41 | Anonymous | 85 | Ray Stanford |
| 41 | Meher Baba | 87 | Anonymous |
| 43 | Meher Baba | 89 | Zoraster |
| 45 | Meher Baba | 91 | Ray Stanford |
| 47 | Meher Baba | | |

# Acknowledgments

All Padmasambhava and Zoroaster quotes reprinted with permission from:
>Twelve World Teachers* by Manly P. Hall.
Los Angeles: Philosophical Research Society, 1965
©copyright Philosophical Research Society

All Lao Tsu quotes from:
*Tao Te Ching* by Lao Tsu
translated by Gia-fu Feng and Jane English
©copyright 1972 by Gia-fu Feng and Jane English
reprinted by permission of Alfred A. Knopf, Inc.

All Buddha quotes from:
*The Dhammapada: The Sayings of the Buddha*
translated by Thomas Byron
©copyright 1976 by Thomas Byron
reprinted by permission of Albert A. Knopf, Inc.

All Meher Baba quotes reprinted with permission from:
*God to Man and Man to God: The Discourses of Meher Baba*
Myrtle Beach, S.C.: Sheriar Press, 1975
©copyright 1975 by Adi K. Irani

All *Miracles* quotes reprinted with permission from:
*A Course in Miracles*
Tiburon, Calif.: The Foundation for Inner Peace, 1975
©copyright 1975, Foundation for Inner Peace, Inc.

All Swami Rama quotes from:
  *Living with the Himalayan Masters* by Swami Rama
  Honesdale, Pa.: Institute of Yoga Science and Philosophy, 1978
  reprinted by permission of the Himalayan Institute Press

All Seth quotes reprinted with permission from:
  *Seth Speaks: the Eternal Validity of the Soul*, by Jane Roberts
  Englewood Cliffs, N.J.: Prentice-Hall, Inc., 1972

All Ray Stanford quotes reprinted with permission from:
  *The Fatima Prophecy*, by Ray Stanford
  New York: Ballantine Books, 1987